The Ultimate Pub Quiz Book

1200 Questions and Answers

ACORN BOOKS

Jack Goldstein

Published in 2016 by
Acorn Books
www.acornbooks.co.uk
an imprint of
Andrews UK Limited
www.andrewsuk.com

All questions and answers in this book are believed
to be correct at the time of printing. If any errors
are found, please inform the publishers, who will be
happy to make corrections to future editions.

Introduction

Thank you for buying this book. Whether you're testing your friends with the odd question here and there, or using it as a basis for your own pub quiz, I hope you find it both useful and enjoyable. I've tried to ensure that there's plenty of variety within these pages, and have included questions at all levels... from the basics that a well-trained chimpanzee should know all the way up to the kind of trivia that would trouble the grand wizard of quizmasters. Good luck, and most of all... have fun!

Jack Goldstein

The Quiz

Questions

Video Game Characters

In which well-known video games did we first come across the following characters?

1. Link

2. Master Chief

3. Lara Croft

4. PiMan

5. Ezio

6. Pikachu

7. Guybrush Threepwood

8. Sackboy

9. Ryu

10. Cloud Strife

Turn to page 126 for the answers

Secret Services

In which country are the following secret service state-run organisations based?

11. Government Communications Security Bureau

12. MI6

13. ASIS

14. Research and Analysis Wing

15. Ministry of State Security

16. Inter-Services Intelligence

17. Mossad

18. Bundesnachrichtendienst

19. Federal Security Service

20. Central Intelligence Agency

Turn to page 127 for the answers

Books with Birds

These books all have a bird in their title – so what is the missing word?

21.   To Kill a ____

22.   Flaubert's ____

23.   Mr Popper's ____

24.   The Maltese ?____

25.   Harry Potter and the Order of the ____

26.   The Ugly ____

27.   Where ____ Dare

28.   One Flew Over the ____ Nest

29.   The ____ Brief

30.   Jonathan Livingston ____

Turn to page 128 for the answers

Band Names

Bands often change their names before hitting the big time. Which famous groups did the following become?

31.   The North London Invaders

32.   Festfolk

33.   Strontium 90

34.   The Moving Sidewalks

35.   Twisted Kites

36.   The Young Aborigines

37.   Johnny and the Moondogs

38.   The Psychedelic Rangers

39.   Smile

40.   The Coventry Automatics

Turn to page 129 for the answers

Mobile Phones

These are some of the best selling mobile phone models of all time. Which company released them?

41. Nexus One

42. 3310

43. Optimus One

44. Z10

45. iPhone

46. W810

47. Desire

48. Galaxy

49. A50

50. Startac

Turn to page 130 for the answers

Famous Scientists

What are the following scientists' first names?

51. Kepler

52. Volta

53. Galilei

54. Watt

55. Newton

56. Einstein

57. Tesla

58. Copernicus

59. Rutherford

60. Marconi

Turn to page 131 for the answers

Instruments

What instrument are the following musicians most famous for playing?

61. John Bonham

62. Dizzy Gillespie

63. Ian Anderson

64. Ravi Shankar

65. Nigel Kennedy

66. Benny Goodman

67. Jimi Hendrix

68. Kenny G

69. Liberace

70. George Formby

Turn to page 132 for the answers

Popes

As of 2014, what is the highest numeral achieved by these papal names?

71. Gregory

72. John

73. Leo

74. Paul

75. John Paul

76. Benedict

77. Innocent

78. Francis

79. Clement

80. Pius

Turn to page 133 for the answers

Capitals and Countries

Of which country are the following cities the capital?

81.   Kabul

82.   Sofia

83.   Ouagadougou

84.   Havana

85.   Cairo

86.   Port-au-Prince

87.   Jerusalem

88.   Beirut

89.   Kathmandu

90.   Abuja

Turn to page 134 for the answers

English Monarchs

Who was England's reigning monarch when these events took place?

91.   The signing of the Magna Carta

92.   England severed its ties with the Catholic Church

93.   The Gunpowder Plot

94.   The Great Fire of London

95.   Slavery abolished in the British Empire

96.   The Great Exhibition

97.   The First World War begins

98.   The Second World War ends

99.   The British humiliate the French at the Battle of Agincourt

100.   Samuel Johnson published the first dictionary

Turn to page 135 for the answers

Shakespeare Quotes

From which Shakespeare play are the following lines taken?

101. Double, double toil and trouble; Fire burn, and cauldron bubble

102. If music be the food of love, play on

103. To be, or not to be: that is the question

104. Is this a dagger which I see before me?

105. Friends, Romans, countrymen, lend me your ears

106. The course of true love never did run smooth

107. Wherefore art thou Romeo?

108. All the world's a stage, and all the men and women merely players

109. Now is the winter of our discontent

110. This above all: to thine own self be true

Turn to page 136 for the answers

Skyscrapers

In which city are the following skyscrapers located?

111. Sears Tower

112. Freedom Tower

113. Ryugyong Hotel

114. Transamerica Pyramid

115. Elephant Tower

116. Burj Khalifa

117. The Gherkin

118. CN Tower

119. Petronas Towers

120. Space Needle

Turn to page 137 for the answers

Football Stadiums

Which football team – or teams – play at the following venues?

121. Bernabéu

122. Old Trafford

123. Karaiskakis Stadium

124. Parc des Princes

125. Camp Nou

126. Petrovsky Stadium

127. Anfield

128. Stadio Olimpico

129. Estádio da Luz

130. Allianz Arena

Turn to page 138 for the answers

Bones

In which part of the human body are the following bones located?

131. Sphenoid

132. Mandible

133. Malleus

134. Humerus

135. Metacarpus

136. Femur

137. Navicular bone

138. Fibula

139. Radius

140. Hyoid

Turn to page 139 for the answers

80s Lyrics

In which songs released in the 1980s will you hear the following lyrics?

141.   Put another dime in the jukebox, baby

142.   Buying bread from a man in Brussels

143.   Tommy used to work on the docks

144.   Who's looking good today? Who's looking good in every way?

145.   I'm killing your brain like a poisonous mushroom

146.   So needless to say of odds and ends

147.   I can't stand this indecision, married with a lack of vision

148.   Clock strikes upon the hour, and the sun begins to fade

149.   I keyed the door, I cold hit the floor, looked up and it was her mother

150.   You end up like a dog that's been beat too much

Turn to page 140 for the answers

Sidekicks

To which famous person are these characters sidekicks?

151.　Waylon Smithers

152.　Sancho Panza

153.　Donkey

154.　Goose

155.　Robin

156.　Pedro Sanchez

157.　Willow Rosenberg

158.　Samwise Gangee

159.　Gromit

160.　Nick Nack

Turn to page 141 for the answers

European Capitals

What is the capital city of the following countries?

161. Slovakia

162. Finland

163. Madrid

164. Belarus

165. Italy

166. Hungary

167. Czech Republic

168. Iceland

169. Austria

170. Cyprus

Turn to page 142 for the answers

Wars

In which century were the following wars fought?

171. The First World War

172. The Napoleonic Wars

173. The An Lushan Rebellion

174. The Thirty Years' War

175. The French Wars of Religion

176. The First Crusade

177. English Civil War

178. American Civil War

179. Inca Civil War

180. The Gothic War

Turn to page 143 for the answers

Children's Books: Part 1

Who is the author of these much-loved children's classics?

181.   The Snowman

182.   The Very Hungry Caterpillar

183.   Where's Spot?

184.   Where the Wild Things Are

185.   The Cat in the Hat

186.   A Bear Called Paddington

187.   Flat Stanley

188.   The BFG

189.   The Queen's Nose

190.   Diary of a Wimpy Kid

Turn to page 144 for the answers

National Football League Teams

In which city or region do the following NFL teams play?

191. Cardinals

192. Seahawks

193. Jaguars

194. Broncos

195. Steelers

196. Titans

197. Lions

198. Chargers

199. Bills

200. Packers

Turn to page 145 for the answers

Dog Breeds

To which breed do the following fictional dogs belong?

201. Santa's Little Helper

202. Beethoven

203. Greyfriars Bobby

204. Digby

205. Lassie

206. Pluto

207. Toto

208. Hooch

209. Scooby Doo

210. Snoopy

Turn to page 146 for the answers

Chemical Elements: Part 1

What is the full name of the following chemical elements?

211. Li

212. Po

213. C

214. Sr

215. I

216. Cl

217. P

218. No

219. Bi

220. Pd

Turn to page 147 for the answers

Lead Singers: Part 1

Who is the lead singer of these bands?

221. Jethro Tull

222. Iron Maiden

223. Mungo Jerry

224. Savage Garden

225. The Stone Roses

226. ZZ Top

227. Metallica

228. Thirty Seconds to Mars

229. Thin Lizzy

230. Dexys Midnight Runners

Turn to page 148 for the answers

Games Consoles

Who manufactured the following consoles?

231. Odyssey

232. Playstation

233. Xbox

234. Jaguar

235. Gamecube

236. Saturn

237. Pippin

238. 2600

239. Vectrex

240. Neo-Geo

Turn to page 149 for the answers

City Nicknames

These are all nicknames of famous cities – but which ones?

241.   Auld Reekie

242.   Motor City

243.   The Fair City

244.   The City of 72 Nations

245.   The Imperial City

246.   The City of Lights

247.   The Windy City

248.   Pearl of the Orient

249.   City of the Kings

250.   The Door to the Dolomites

Turn to page 150 for the answers

Political Parties

Of which political party were the following people leaders?

251. Nigel Farage

252. Geoffrey Clements

253. David Sutch

254. Caroline Lucas

255. Paddy Ashdown

256. Alasdair McDonnell

257. Gerry Adams

258. David Owen

259. Neville Chamberlain

260. Clement Attlee

Turn to page 151 for the answers

Cartoon Baddies

In which cartoon did the following baddies appear?

261.   Baron von Greenback

262.   Sideshow Bob

263.   Skeletor

264.   Gargamel

265.   Venger

266.   Zoltar

267.   Dr. Von Goosewing

268.   Doctor Claw

269.   Megatron

270.   Mumm-ra

Turn to page 152 for the answers

Sports à la Française

These are all well-known sports, but in French. What do we call them in English?

271. Le ski nautique

272. La voile

273. Le patinage

274. La lutte

275. Le tir à l'arc

276. La boxe

277. Le cyclisme

278. La natation

279. La plongée

280. La pêche

Turn to page 153 for the answers

Film Decades

The following films won 'best picture' at the Oscars, but in which decade?

281.   Rocky

282.   Casablanca

283.   Gladiator

284.   Braveheart

285.   All Quiet on the Western Front

286.   The King's Speech

287.   The Sound of Music

288.   Gandhi

289.   The Bridge on the River Kwai

290.   Wings

Turn to page 154 for the answers

Young Animals: Part 1

What are the young of the following animals called?

291. Deer

292. Cat

293. Bee

294. Turkey

295. Kangaroo

296. Antelope

297. Fly

298. Goose

299. Fish

300. Crocodile

Turn to page 155 for the answers

Famous Albums: Part 1

Which artists released these albums, considered some of the greatest of all time?

301.   Rumours

302.   Kind of Blue

303.   The Joshua Tree

304.   Sgt. Pepper's Lonely Hearts Club Band

305.   Astral Weeks

306.   Exile on Main Street

307.   Nevermind

308.   London Calling

309.   Highway 61 Revisited

310.   Innervisons

Turn to page 156 for the answers

Detectives

These characters helped solve various crimes – but what are their day jobs?

311.   Mark Sloan

312.   Quincy

313.   Jonathan Creek

314.   Shoestring

315.   Jessica Fletcher

316.   Cadfael

317.   Patrick Jane

318.   Lovejoy

319.   Petrocelli

320.   Rosemary & Thyme

Turn to page 157 for the answers

Lakes

In which country are these lakes situated?

321. Annecy

322. Garda

323. Windermere

324. Sognefjord

325. Bled

326. Lucerne

327. Saimaa

328. Hallstattersee

329. Konigsee

330. Onega

Turn to page 158 for the answers

American Presidents

Who was president of the USA when these famous events happened?

331. The Space Shuttle *Challenger* explodes

332. A nuclear bomb is dropped on Hiroshima

333. The Vietnam War ends

334. Man lands on the moon for the first time

335. Terrorists fly two hijacked planes into the World Trade Center

336. Thirteenth Amendment to the United States Constitution is adopted, abolishing slavery

337. The US buys 828,000 square miles of land in Louisiana from France

338. America declares war against the British Empire

339. Black Tuesday signifies the beginning of the great depression

340. Japanese forces launch a surprise attack against Pearl Harbour

Turn to page 159 for the answers

Original Languages

Which language were the following books first written in?

341.   The Girl with the Dragon Tattoo

342.   Around the World in Eighty Days

343.   Anna Karenina

344.   All Quiet on the Western Front

345.   Love in the Time of Cholera

346.   The Metamorphosis

347.   The Unbearable Lightness of Being

348.   Snow Country

349.   The Silence of the Lambs

350.   The Three Musketeers

Turn to page 160 for the answers

Grand Prix Circuits

In which country will you find these circuits that at one time or another have hosted a Formula 1 Grand Prix?

351. Silverstone

352. Circuit Gilles Villeneuve

353. Hockenheimring

354. Red Bull Ring

355. Suzuka Circuit

356. Kyalami

357. Circuit Park Zandvoort

358. Autódromo Hermanos Rodríguez

359. Circuit Paul Ricard

360. Yas Marina Circuit

Turn to page 161 for the answers

International Currencies: Part 1

As of 2014, what is the standard currency of the following countries?

361.   Bulgaria

362.   Costa Rica

363.   Italy

364.   New Zealand

365.   Russia

366.   South Africa

367.   Thailand

368.   Vietnam

369.   Zambia

370.   Estonia

Turn to page 162 for the answers

Measurements

What are the following units used to measure?

371. Newton

372. Coulomb

373. Ohm

374. Weber

375. Radian

376. Pascal

377. Henry

378. Sievert

379. Lux

380. Katal

Turn to page 163 for the answers

21st Century Song Lyrics

In which well-known songs released after the year 2000 can you find these lyrics?

381.   I'm noddin' my head like yeah, movin' my hips like yeah

382.   Can't read my, can't read my, no he can't read my...

383.   She had dumps like a truck truck truck, thighs like what what what

384.   Boys getting high and the girls even more so

385.   You're my experimental game, just human nature

386.   Since the last time you heard from me I lost some friends; well, hell, me and Snoop, we dipping again

387.   You thought that I'd be weak without you but I'm stronger

388.   I wanna kiss you every minute, every hour, every day

389.   Yellow cab, gypsy cab, dollar cab, holla back

390.   We'll get her jacked up on some cheap champagne, we'll let the good times all roll out

Turn to page 164 for the answers

Disney Songs

In which Disney film will you find these songs?

391.   Whistle While you Work

392.   When I See an Elephant Fly

393.   Give a Little Whistle

394.   Never Smile at a Crocodile

395.   Friends on the Other Side

396.   The Phony King of England

397.   Part of Your World

398.   Something There

399.   One Jump Ahead

400.   Topsy Turvy

Turn to page 165 for the answers

Internet Domains

The following internet domain suffixes belong to which countries?

401. .at

402. .cr

403. .vu

404. .se

405. .no

406. .mc

407. .hn

408. .fj

409. .bg

410. .za

Turn to page 166 for the answers

Greek Gods

Who was the ancient Greek god of...

411. Love

412. The Underworld

413. Women & Childbirth

414. The Sea

415. The Sky, Weather and Thunder

416. The Home

417. Travel

418. Metalworking

419. Wine

420. Agriculture

Turn to page 167 for the answers

Year of Publication

In which year were the following literary works first published?

421.   A Clockwork Orange

422.   Wuthering Heights

423.   To Kill a Mockingbird

424.   The Hobbit

425.   Dracula

426.   The Adventures of Huckleberry Finn

427.   The Catcher in the Rye

428.   Lord of the Flies

429.   The Da Vinci Code

430.   Alice's Adventures in Wonderland

Turn to page 168 for the answers

Cars: Part 1

Which manufacturer is most famous for the following cars?

431. Fuego

432. Cavalier

433. Cherokee

434. 911

435. NSX

436. 2CV

437. Uno

438. Golf

439. Polonez

440. Firebird

Turn to page 169 for the answers

Major League Baseball

These are all nicknames of MLB teams — but where are they based?

441. Braves

442. Red Sox

443. Pirates

444. Rangers

445. Brewers

446. Mariners

447. Cardinals

448. Orioles

449. Marlins

450. Blue Jays

Turn to page 170 for the answers

Chemical Elements: Part 2

As before, what is the full name of the following chemical elements?

451.   Pb

452.   Cu

453.   K

454.   Sn

455.   Na

456.   F

457.   Fe

458.   Mn

459.   Kr

460.   H

Turn to page 171 for the answers

Food Songs

Here are some songs with various foodstuffs in their titles. Which group or artist is most famous for singing them?

461.   Glass Onion

462.   Cornflake Girl

463.   I Want Candy

464.   Strange Fruit

465.   Mouldy Old Dough

466.   American Pie

467.   Blueberry Hill

468.   Brown Sugar

469.   Toast

470.   Pour Some Sugar On Me

Turn to page 172 for the answers

Great Works of Art

Who painted the following great works?

471. The Birth of Venus

472. Water Lillies

473. Night Watch

474. The Scream

475. The Girl with a Pearl Earring

476. Guernica

477. The Creation of Adam

478. The Last Supper

479. Starry Night

480. The Persistence Of Memory

Turn to page 173 for the answers

Capital Cities of Asia

Of which countries are the following cities the capitals?

481. Phnom Penh

482. Vientiane

483. Kathmandu

484. Thimphu

485. Ulaanbaatar

486. Pyongyang

487. Taipei

488. Naypyidaw

489. Dili

490. Colombo

Turn to page 174 for the answers

Leaders' Wives

To which American President were each of these women married?

491. Lady Bird Taylor

492. Martha Dandridge

493. Lucretia Rudolph

494. Mary Todd

495. Grace Anna Goodhue

496. Louisa Johnson

497. Eleanor Smith

498. Edith Carow

499. Jacqueline Bouvier

500. Michelle Robinson

Turn to page 175 for the answers

Anagrams: Part 1

These are anagrams of well-known authors. Can you un-scramble them?

501. Hens Kept Gin

502. Aha Tragic Heist

503. My Thinner Sewage

504. Leases Imperial Hawk

505. Me Raging Terror

506. A Slow Cider

507. Licks Jail Once

508. Gonadal Repeal

509. Nae Just Nae

510. He Licks Dancers

Turn to page 176 for the answers

Winter Olympic Sports

These are all sports that have in recent years appeared in the winter Olympics. Each '–' represents a letter... so what are they?

511. S-------

512. B--------

513. N----- C-------

514. C------

515. B-------

516. A----- S-----

517. S-- J------

518. L---

519. I-- H-----

520. F----- S------

Turn to page 177 for the answers

Museums

In which city will you find the following museums?

521.   Rijksmuseum

522.   Prado Museum

523.   Museo Nacional de Antropologia

524.   National Palace Museum

525.   Uffizi Gallery

526.   Metropolitan Museum of Art

527.   Louvre

528.   Tate Modern

529.   Pergamonmuseum

530.   Belvedere

Turn to page 178 for the answers

Measuring Devices

What are the following devices designed to measure?

531. Hygrometer

532. Chronometer

533. Cathetometer

534. Fathometer

535. Barometer

536. Anemometer

537. Manometer

538. Tintometer

539. Odometer

540. Sphygmomanometer

Turn to page 179 for the answers

Famous Albums: Part 2

Name the artists responsible for these best-selling albums...

541. Superfly

542. It Takes a Nation of Millions to Hold Us Back

543. Odessey and Oracle

544. The Rise and Fall of Ziggy Stardust and the Spiders From Mars

545. Trout Mask Replica

546. Horses

547. Electric Ladyland

548. Legend

549. Forever Changes

550. Kid A

Turn to page 180 for the answers

Flag Carriers

For which countries are these airlines the flag carriers?

551.   Copa Airlines

552.   Etihad Airways

553.   Aer Lingus

554.   Avianca

555.   Aeroflot

556.   Gulf Air

557.   El Al

558.   Qantas

559.   Air Baltic

560.   Iberia

Turn to page 181 for the answers

Volcanoes

In which country are the following Volcanoes situated?

561. Chimborazo

562. Kilimanjaro

563. El Misti

564. Popocatépetl

565. Ararat

566. Churchill

567. Fuji

568. Etna

569. Silverthrone

570. Elbrus

Turn to page 182 for the answers

Leaders in War

In which war did the following great generals and leaders fight, and for which 'side'?

571. Patton

572. Grant

573. Lee

574. Yamamoto

575. Schwarzkopf

576. Hannibal

577. Cyrus

578. Alexander

579. Napoleon Bonaparte

580. William the Conqueror

Turn to page 183 for the answers

Authors

Who wrote the following great literary works?

581. Sense and Sensibility

582. Don Quixote

583. The Great Gatsby

584. Of Mice and Men

585. War and Peace

586. Mein Kampf

587. Gulliver's Travels

588. The Canterbury Tales

589. Moby Dick

590. The Trial

Turn to page 184 for the answers

Previously Known As...

Which famous people were originally called:

591. Maurice Micklewhite

592. Allen Konigsberg

593. Ehrich Weiss

594. Georgios Panayiotou

595. Natalie Herschlag

596. Frances Gumm

597. Steveland Judkins

598. Katy Hudson

599. Norma Jean Mortensen

600. Caryn Johnson

Turn to page 185 for the answers

Olympic Cities

Who hosted the summer Olympics in the following years?

601. 1976

602. 1980

603. 2004

604. 1960

605. 1936

606. 2012

607. 1952

608. 1900

609. 1928

610. 1988

Turn to page 186 for the answers

SI Units

What is the SI unit for...

611.   Electric Current

612.   Power

613.   Time

614.   Mass

615.   Radioactivity

616.   Temperature

617.   Length

618.   Frequency

619.   Magnetic Field Strength

620.   Capacitance

Turn to page 187 for the answers

Nationalities of Singers

Which nationality are the following well-known singers?

621. Bryan Adams

622. Kylie Minogue

623. Bjork

624. Tim Finn

625. Nena

626. Demis Roussos

627. Grace Jones

628. Shreya Ghoshal

629. Youssou N'dour

630. PSY

Turn to page 188 for the answers

Famous Battles

In which year were these battles fought?

631.   Battle of Marathon

632.   Battle of Hastings

633.   Battle of Blenheim

634.   Battle of Gaugamela

635.   Battle of Waterloo

636.   Battle of Midway

637.   Battle of Gettysburg

638.   Battle of Tours

639.   Battle of the Somme

640.   Battle of Agincourt

Turn to page 189 for the answers

Nicknames of Countries

These are often-used nicknames of countries across the world, but to where do they refer?

641.   Land of Hope and Glory

642.   The Bread Basket of Europe

643.   The Red Dragon

644.   India's Teardrop

645.   Land of the Long White Cloud

646.   The Gift of the Nile

647.   The Red Island

648.   The Emerald Isle

649.   Uncle Sam

650.   Land of Fire and Ice

Turn to page 190 for the answers

Mythical Creatures

Classical mythology is full of fantastic and unusual creatures; what is being described by the following?

651. The head of a bull on the body of a man

652. A pure white winged stallion

653. The head and torso of a human on the body of a horse

654. Three women with snakes for hair whose gaze would turn you to stone

655. Giant with one eye

656. Multi-headed guard dog of the underworld

657. An eagle's head, wings and front feet with the back end of a lion

658. Enchanting women who would lure sailors to their deaths on the rocks

659. The face of a woman, the wings of a great bird and the hindquarters of a lion.

660. Half-woman, half-snake, the mother of all monsters

Turn to page 191 for the answers

Literary Characters: Part 1

In which famous works were the following characters first found?

661. George Smiley

662. Draco Malfoy

663. Big Brother

664. Shere Khan

665. Sauron

666. Zaphod Beeblebrox

667. Algernon Moncrieff

668. Captain Ahab

669. The Wife of Bath

670. Katniss Everdeen

Turn to page 192 for the answers

Team Numbers

How many players are there (in play) for a team in each of the following sports?

671. Association Football (Soccer)

672. Basketball

673. Rugby Union

674. Curling

675. Netball

676. Cricket

677. Ice Hockey

678. Tug-of-war

679. Hurling

680. Men's Lacrosse

Turn to page 193 for the answers

Horror Movies

In which horror movie did we first meet these terrifying characters?

681. Freddy Krueger

682. Leatherface

683. Pinhead

684. Jason Voorhees

685. Damien Thorn

686. Michael Myers

687. Norman Bates

688. Samara

689. Captain Spaulding

690. Pennywise

Turn to page 194 for the answers

Moons

Around which planet do the following moons orbit?

691. Luna

692. Phobos

693. Callisto

694. Europa

695. Hyperion

696. Calypso

697. Cressida

698. Triton

699. Charon

700. Oberon

Turn to page 195 for the answers

Notes and Keys

For the first five questions, how many standard beats do the notes last for. For the second five questions, which sharps or flats are used for the key?

701.   Quaver

702.   Minim

703.   Semibreve

704.   Semiquaver

705.   Crotchet

706.   G major

707.   E flat minor

708.   E major

709.   B flat major

710.   C minor

Turn to page 196 for the answers

Movie Taglines

These are all taglines from famous movies – but which ones?

711. In space no one can hear you scream

712. Be afraid. Be very afraid.

713. One dream. Four Jamaicans. Twenty below zero.

714. We are not alone

715. What kind of man would defy a king?

716. On every street in every city, there's a nobody who dreams of being a somebody

717. Just when you thought it was safe to go back in the water

718. Are you watching closely?

719. The future is history

720. Earth - take a good look. It could be your last.

Turn to page 197 for the answers

State Capitals

What are the capitals of the following American states?

721.   Maryland

722.   Illinois

723.   Florida

724.   Oregon

725.   Louisiana

726.   Arizona

727.   Hawaii

728.   Texas

729.   Utah

730.   Nebraska

Turn to page 198 for the answers

Parliament Buildings

These are all uniquely-named parliament buildings; in which countries are they situated?

731. Binnenhof

732. Palais du Peuple

733. Palais Bourbon

734. Reichstag

735. Sansad Bhavan

736. Leinster House

737. The Red House

738. Christiansborg Palace

739. Great Hall of the People

740. Tintenpalast

Turn to page 199 for the answers

Eras of Art

In which era or school were these artists most prominent?

741.   Sandro Botticelli

742.   Pablo Picasso

743.   John Everett Millais

744.   Gustave Courbet

745.   Rembrandt

746.   Jacques-Louis David

747.   Marcel Duchamp

748.   François Boucher

749.   Claude Monet

750.   Caspar David Friedrich

Turn to page 200 for the answers

Acronyms

What do these sporting acronyms commonly stand for?

751.   MLB

752.   OG

753.   LPGA

754.   IOC

755.   FIFA

756.   DNF

757.   AVG

758.   TKO

759.   XC

760.   QB

Turn to page 201 for the answers

Serial Killers

What nickname has been given to these well-known serial killers?

761. John George Haigh

762. Harold Shipman

763. Keith Hunter Jesperson

764. Ed Gein

765. Albert Fish

766. Andrei Chikatilo

767. Ian Brady & Myra Hindley

768. John Wayne Gacy

769. Peter Sutcliffe

770. Albert DeSalvo

Turn to page 202 for the answers

Moonwalkers

All of these men have walked on the moon – but as part of which Apollo missions?

771.   James Irwin

772.   David Scott

773.   Alan Shepard

774.   Alan Bean

775.   Pete Conrad

776.   Neil Armstrong

777.   John W Young

778.   Harrison Schmitt

779.   Charles Duke

780.   Eugene Cernan

Turn to page 203 for the answers

Symphonies

Which classical composers wrote the following symphonies?

781. Roméo et Juliette

782. Faust Symphony

783. Unfinished

784. Fire Symphony

785. Jupiter

786. Resurrection Symphony

787. Eroica

788. Babi Yar

789. A London Symphony

790. Pathétique

Turn to page 204 for the answers

Sitcoms

In which cities or locations are these famous comedies set?

791.   Happy Days

792.   The Office (US)

793.   Roseanna

794.   Family Guy

795.   Frasier

796.   Cheers

797.   Fawtly Towers

798.   Friends

799.   Only Fools and Horses

800.   M*A*S*H

Turn to page 205 for the answers

Famous Landmarks

In which city will you find the following well-known landmarks?

801. Statue of Liberty

802. Eiffel Tower

803. Little Mermaid

804. Taj Mahal

805. Christ the Redeemer

806. Hagia Sophia

807. Sagrada Familia

808. Manneken Pis

809. St. Peter's Cathedral

810. Al Aqsa Mosque

Turn to page 206 for the answers

Calendar Dates

On which date of the year do the following days fall?

811. Armistice Day

812. The Ides of March

813. New Year's Day

814. Australia Day

815. St George's Day (in the UK)

816. Star Wars Day

817. Canada Day

818. Hallowe'en

819. Guy Fawkes Night

820. Valentine's Day

Turn to page 207 for the answers

Bible Quotes

In which book of the bible will you find the following?

821.   In the beginning, God created the heavens and the earth.

822.   You shall have no other gods before me.

823.   And I tell you, ask, and it will be given to you; seek, and you will find; knock, and it will be opened to you.

824.   For God so loved the world, that he gave his only Son, that whoever believes in him should not perish but have eternal life.

825.   So now faith, hope, and love abide, these three; but the greatest of these is love.

826.   In all thy ways acknowledge him, and he shall direct thy paths.

827.   Even though I walk through the darkest valley, I will fear no evil, for you are with me; your rod and your staff, they comfort me.

828. I can do all things through Christ who strengthens me.

829. Be strong and courageous. Do not be afraid or terrified because of them, for the Lord your God goes with you; he will never leave you nor forsake you.

830. Consider the lilies of the field, how they grow; they toil not, neither do they spin.

Turn to page 208 for the answers

Winter Olympics

Where were the Winter Olympics held in the following years?

831. 1948

832. 2014

833. 2002

834. 1994

835. 1988

836. 1984

837. 1976

838. 1952

839. 1924

840. 2010

Turn to page 209 for the answers

Cars: Part 2

And again, which manufacturer is most famous for the following cars?

841. FTO

842. Lagonda

843. Escalade

844. Viper

845. Enzo

846. XJS

847. Miura

848. Defender

849. Interceptor

850. Vel Satis

Turn to page 210 for the answers

Scientists

Which scientist is most famous for proposing the following theories, discoveries or principles?

851.   Gravity

852.   The Uncertainty Principle

853.   General Relativity

854.   Evolution

855.   Planetary Motion

856.   The Buoyancy Principle

857.   Antibiotics (Penicillin)

858.   The Law of Induction

859.   Insulin

860.   Radioactivity

Turn to page 211 for the answers

Songs with Colours

Who is best known for the following hit singles?

861.   Blue Monday

862.   A Whiter Shade of Pale

863.   Golden Brown

864.   99 Red Balloons

865.   Purple Haze

866.   Orange Crush

867.   I See Red

868.   White Room

869.   Black Hole Sun

870.   Blueberry Hill

Turn to page 212 for the answers

Archenemies

Of which character (or group of characters) are the following the archenemy of?

871. Black Manta

872. Kingpin

873. Magneto

874. The Joker

875. Lex Luthor

876. Red Skull

877. Doctor Doom

878. Loki

879. Mandarin

880. Sinestro

Turn to page 213 for the answers

Rivers

Around which rivers are the following capital cities built?

881.   Washington D.C.

882.   Buenos Aries

883.   Vienna

884.   Beijing

885.   London

886.   Paris

887.   Baghdad

888.   Rome

889.   Amsterdam

890.   Khartoum

Turn to page 214 for the answers

European Monarchs

Who was monarch of the following European countries at the turn of the millennium?

891.   Belgium

892.   Denmark

893.   Liechtenstein

894.   Luxembourg

895.   Monaco

896.   Netherlands

897.   Norway

898.   Spain

899.   Sweden

900.   United Kingdom

Turn to page 215 for the answers

Opening Lines

These are the opening lines to famous literary works... but which ones?

901.   It is a truth universally acknowledged, that a single man in possession of a good fortune, must be in want of a wife.

902.   It was the best of times, it was the worst of times.

903.   It was a bright cold day in April, and the clocks were striking thirteen.

904.   riverrun, past Eve and Adam's, from swerve of shore to bend of bay, brings us by a commodius vicus of recirculation back to Howth Castle and Environs.

905.   In my younger and more vulnerable years my father gave me some advice that I've been turning over in my mind ever since.

906.   Call me Ishmael.

907.   All children, except one, grow up.

908.   All this happened, more or less.

909. Mr. and Mrs. Dursley of number four Privet Drive were proud to say that they were perfectly normal, thank you very much.

910. We were somewhere around Barstow on the edge of the desert when the drugs began to take hold.

Turn to page 216 for the answers

Movie Characters

Which movies first featured the following famous characters?

911. Vito Corleone

912. Norman Bates

913. Ellen Ripley

914. Randle Patrick McMurphy

915. Peter Marwood

916. Dorothy Gale

917. Travis Bickle

918. Gordon Gekko

919. Jules Winnfield

920. Alex DeLarge

Turn to page 217 for the answers

Sports Trophies

Here are the names of some famous trophies... but teams and individuals from which sports compete for them?

921.   Stanley Cup

922.   Leonard Trophy

923.   Vince Lombardi Trophy

924.   Davis Cup

925.   Bledisloe Cup

926.   Borg-Warner Trophy

927.   Claret Jug

928.   America's Cup

929.   Ashes

930.   Prince Rainar Cup

Turn to page 218 for the answers

Phobias

What are people with the following phobias terrified of?

931.   Arachnophobia

932.   Scotophobia

933.   Ichthyophobia

934.   Ornithophobia

935.   Pogonophobia

936.   Sciophobia

937.   Limnophobia

938.   Claustrophobia

939.   Phasmophobia

940.   Ailurophobia

Turn to page 219 for the answers

Sporting Locations

What famous sporting events take place in the following locations?

941.　Kentucky

942.　Indianapolis

943.　Wimbledon

944.　Aintree

945.　St Andrews

946.　Augusta

947.　Wembley

948.　Le Mans

949.　Cowes

950.　Monaco

Turn to page 220 for the answers

Inventions

Who is commonly considered* to be the inventor of the following?

951.　Telephone

952.　World Wide Web

953.　Cotton Gin

954.　Steam Engine

955.　Printing Press

956.　The Television

957.　Bifocal Glasses

958.　Spinning Jenny

959.　Hovercraft

960.　Cats Eyes

Turn to page 221 for the answers

*Note: the author is aware that some of these are disputed.

Deserts

Name at least one of the countries in which the following deserts are located...

961.   Dungeness

962.   Oleshky Sands

963.   Simpson

964.   Tabernas

965.   Atacama

966.   Kalahari

967.   Gobi

968.   Negev

969.   Indus Valley

970.   Patagonian

Turn to page 222 for the answers

Revolutionaries

These men either led or assisted significant revolutions in their home countries. But which countries are they?

971. Mustafa Kamal Attaturk

972. William Wallace

973. Mao Zedong

974. Ayotullah Khomeini

975. Michael Collins

976. Oliver Cromwell

977. Giuseppe Garibaldi

978. Fidel Castro

979. Sri Aurobindo

980. Maximilien Robespierre

Turn to page 223 for the answers

Anagrams: Part 2

Some detective work is required to decipher these anagrams of well-known mystery solvers...

981.   Chokes Her Molls

982.   Employed Writers

983.   Cool Bum

984.   Limp Smears

985.   Speculation Course

986.   Our Helicopter

987.   Dames Sap

988.   Overuse And More

989.   Year Old Cigar

990.   Her Brown Fat

Turn to page 224 for the answers

Famous Olympians

These Olympians are some of the most successful in their individual disciplines, which are...?

991. Edoardo Mangiarotti

992. Pyrros Dimas

993. Kim Soo-nyung

994. Steve Redgrave

995. Tadahiro Nomura

996. Michael Phelps

997. Ben Ainslie

998. Larisa Latynina

999. Chris Hoy

1000. Birgit Fischer

Turn to page 225 for the answers

Gemstones

What basic colour (most commonly) are the following gemstones?

1001. Peridot

1002. Topaz

1003. Moonstone

1004. Amethyst

1005. Garnet

1006. Onyx

1007. Emerald

1008. Citrine

1009. Tanzanite

1010. Ruby

Turn to page 226 for the answers

Young Animals: Part 2

Again, what is the common name for the juveniles of these animals?

1011. Ferret

1012. Cicada

1013. Llama

1014. Swan

1015. Bear

1016. Hare

1017. Horse

1018. Hawk

1019. Goat

1020. Eel

Turn to page 227 for the answers

Musical Nicknames

Some musicians acquire rather lofty titles during and after their careers. To whom do the following monikers refer?

1021. Mr. Eurovision

1022. The Prince of Darkness

1023. The Godfather of Britpop

1024. The Godfather of Soul

1025. The King of Calypso

1026. The King of Pop

1027. The Boss

1028. The Forces' Sweetheart

1029. The King of Swing

1030. The Modfather

Turn to page 228 for the answers

Bridges

In which city do these bridges stand?

1031. Brooklyn Bridge

1032. Rialto Bridge

1033. Stari Most

1034. Charles Bridge

1035. Tower Bridge

1036. Golden Gate Bridge

1037. Vasco da Gama Bridge

1038. Ponte Vecchio

1039. Royal Gorge Bridge

1040. Si-o-se Pol

Turn to page 229 for the answers

Countries and Capitals

What is the capital city of the following countries?

1041. Belgium

1042. China

1043. Croatia

1044. Denmark

1045. Germany

1046. Iceland

1047. Indonesia

1048. South Korea

1049. Peru

1050. Turkey

Turn to page 230 for the answers

Roman Gods

Who was the ancient Roman god of...

1051. Wisdom

1052. The Home

1053. Women & Childbirth

1054. Agriculture

1055. The Moon

1056. Love

1057. War

1058. The Sra

1059. Fire

1060. The Sky, Weather and Thunder

Turn to page 231 for the answers

Literary Characters: Part 2

In which famous works can the following characters be found?

1061. Pip

1062. Inigo Montoya

1063. Humbert Humbert

1064. Yossarian

1065. Atticus Finch,

1066. Toad

1067. Fitzwilliam Darcy

1068. Anne Shirley

1069. Mark Renton

1070. Jack Torrance

Turn to page 232 for the answers

International Currencies: Part 2

Again, as of 2014, what is the standard currency of the following countries?

1071. Iraq

1072. Brazil

1073. Denmark

1074. Guatemala

1075. India

1076. Japan

1077. South Korea

1078. Malaysia

1079. Poland

1080. Kenya

Turn to page 233 for the answers

World Cup Hosts

Who were the hosts of the FIFA world cup in the following years?

1081. 1978

1082. 1966

1083. 1954

1084. 1962

1085. 1938

1086. 1930

1087. 2010

1088. 1986

1089. 1950

1090. 2002

Turn to page 234 for the answers

Chemical Elements: Part 3

Once again, what is the full name of the following chemical elements?

1091. Hg

1092. Es

1093. Yb

1094. As

1095. Sb

1096. Ba

1097. W

1098. Pu

1099. Hs

1100. Ag

Turn to page 235 for the answers

90s Lyrics

In which songs released in the 1990s can you hear the following lyrics?

1101. Where did you come from, where did you go?

1102. Hangin' out the passenger side of his best friend's ride

1103. A licky boom-boom down

1104. You're licking your lips and blowing kisses my way

1105. There used to be a graying tower alone on the sea

1106. Nobody likes you when you're 23

1107. You'll never know how I watched you from the shadows as a child

1108. Take me to the magic of the moment on a glory night

1109. Yo back up now and give a brother room

1110. Extraordinary, juice like a strawberry, money to burn baby, all of the time

Turn to page 236 for the answers

Country Names

These are the names of some countries but in their native language. What do we call them in English?

1111. Nippon

1112. Kalaallit Nunaat

1113. Deutschland

1114. Sverige

1115. Suomi

1116. Österreich

1117. Hrvatska

1118. Sesel

1119. Viti

Magyarország

Turn to page 237 for the answers

African Capitals

Of which African country are the following cities the capital?

1120. Addis Ababa

1121. Dakar

1122. Kampala

1123. Mogadishu

1124. Algiers

1125. Dar es Salaam

1126. Harare

1127. Nairobi

1128. Freetown

1129. Rabat

Turn to page 238 for the answers

Famous Leaders

Which country (or empire) did the following people lead?

1130. Adolf Hitler

1131. The Dalai Lama

1132. Constantine the Great

1133. Mustafa Kemal Atatürk

1134. Genghis Khan

1135. Charlemagne

1136. Frederick the Great

1137. Saladin

1138. Attila

1139. Hammurabi

Turn to page 239 for the answers

Children's Books: Part 2

Once again, who is the author of these much-loved children's classics?

1140. Winnie-the-Pooh

1141. The Worst Witch

1142. Charlotte's Web

1143. Artemis Fowl

1144. Stig of the Dump

1145. The Lion, the Witch and the Wardrobe

1146. The Borrowers

1147. Harry Potter and the Philosopher's Stone

1148. Watership Down

1149. Stormbreaker

Turn to page 240 for the answers

Football Nicknames

Which association football (soccer) teams are also known by the following nicknames?

1150. Blades

1151. Cherries

1152. Grecians

1153. Gunners

1154. Owls

1155. Pirates

1156. Posh

1157. Railwaymen

1158. Seagulls

1159. Tractor Boys

Turn to page 241 for the answers

Computer Acronyms

What do the following technology-related acronyms stand for?

1160. ASCII

1161. BASIC

1162. CPU

1163. DNS

1164. GUI

1165. HTTP

1166. IM

1167. P2P

1168. PC

1169. USB

Turn to page 242 for the answers

Collective Nouns

What is the commonly-used collective noun for the following?

1170. Apes

1171. Wild Boars

1172. Caterpillars

1173. Dolphins

1174. Lions

1175. Owls

1176. Vipers

1177. Woodpeckers

1178. Crows

1179. Dogs

Turn to page 243 for the answers

Lead Singers: Part 2

For which band are these people lead singer?

1180. Brian Johnson

1181. Richard Fairbrass

1182. Billie Joe Armstrong

1183. Matthew Bellamy

1184. Jarvis Cocker

1185. Mark Knopfler

1186. Jas Mann

1187. Marti Pellow

1188. Gwen Stefani

1189. Steven Tyler

Turn to page 244 for the answers

Catchphrases

On which UK TV show will you hear...

1190. No likey no lighty

1191. Ooh, you are awful... but I like you

1192. They don't like it up 'em!

1193. You dirty old man

1194. Listen very carefully, I shall say this only once

1195. Calm down! Calm down!

1196. Computer says no

1197. I've started so I'll finish

1198. Smoke me a kipper, I'll be back for breakfast

1199. Ooh I could crush a grape

Turn to page 245 for the answers

Answers

Video Game Characters

1. The Legend of Zelda

2. Halo

3. Tomb Raider

4. Pimania

5. Assassin's Creed II

6. Pokemon Red/Green

7. The Secret of Monkey Island

8. LittleBigPlanet

9. Street Fighter

10. Final Fantasy VII

Secret Services

11. New Zealand

12. United Kingdom

13. Australia

14. India

15. China

16. Pakistan

17. Israel

18. Germany

19. Russia

20. USA

Books with Birds

21.   Mockingbird

22.   Parrot

23.   Penguins

24.   Falcon

25.   Phoenix

26.   Duckling

27.   Eagles

28.   Cuckoo's

29.   Pelican

30.   Seagull

Band Names

31. Madness

32. Abba

33. The Police

34. ZZ Top

35. R.E.M.

36. The Beastie Boys

37. The Beatles

38. The Doors

39. Queen

40. The Specials

Mobile Phones

41.   Google

42.   Nokia

43.   LG

44.   Blackberry (RIM)

45.   Apple

46.   Sony Ericsson

47.   HTC

48.   Samsung

49.   Siemens

50.   Motorola

Famous Scientists

51. Johannes

52. Alessandro

53. Galileo

54. James

55. Isaac

56. Albert

57. Nikola

58. Nicolaus

59. Ernest

60. Guglielmo

Instruments

61. Drums (Percussion)

62. Trumpet

63. Flute - and also guitar (acoustic), keyboards, bass guitar, bouzouki, balalaika, saxophone, harmonica, and a variety of whistles.

64. Sitar

65. Violin

66. Clarinet

67. Guitar (Electric)

68. Saxophone

69. Piano

70. Ukulele

Popes

71. XVI

72. XXIII

73. XIII

74. VI

75. II

76. XVI

77. XIII

78. I

79. XIV

80. XII

Capitals and Countries

81.   Afghanistan

82.   Bulgaria

83.   Burkina Faso

84.   Cuba

85.   Egypt

86.   Haiti

87.   Israel

88.   Lebanon

89.   Nepal

90.   Nigeria

English Monarchs

91.   King John (1215)

92.   Henry VIII (1529)

93.   James I (1605)

94.   Charles II (1666)

95.   William IV (1833)

96.   Victoria (1851)

97.   George V (1914)

98.   George VI (1945)

99.   Henry V (1415)

100.   George II (1755)

Shakespeare Quotes

101.   Macbeth

102.   Twelfth Night

103.   Hamlet

104.   Macbeth

105.   Julius Caesar

106.   A Misdummer Night's Dream

107.   Romeo and Juliet

108.   As you Like It

109.   Richard III

110.   Hamlet

Skyscrapers

111. Chicago

112. New York

113. Pyongyang

114. San Francisco

115. Bangkok

116. Dubai

117. London

118. Toronto

119. Kuala Lumpur

120. Seattle

Football Stadiums

121. Real Madrid

122. Manchester United

123. Olympiacos

124. Paris St German

125. Barcelona

126. Zenit Saint Petersburg

127. Liverpool

128. Lazio / Roma

129. Benfica

130. Bayern Munich

Bones

131. Head

132. Face

133. Ear

134. Arm

135. Hand

136. Leg

137. Foot

138. Leg

139. Arm

140. Throat

80s Lyrics

141. I Love Rock'N'Roll

142. Down Under

143. Livin' on a Prayer

144. Buffalo Stance

145. Ice Ice Baby

146. Take On Me

147. Everybody Wants to Rule the World

148. I Wanna Dance with Somebody

149. Wild Thing

150. Born in the USA

Sidekicks

151. Mr Burns

152. Don Quixote

153. Shrek

154. Maverick

155. Batman

156. Napoleon Dynamite

157. Buffy the Vampire Slayer

158. Frodo Baggins

159. Wallace

160. Francisco Scaramanga

European Capitals

161. Bratislava

162. Helsinki

163. Spain

164. Minsk

165. Rome

166. Budapest

167. Prague

168. Reykjavik

169. Vienna

170. Nicosia

Wars

171. 20th

172. 19th

173. 8th

174. 17th

175. 16th

176. 11th

177. 17th

178. 19th

179. 16th

180. 4th

Children's Books: Part 1

181.   Raymond Briggs

182.   Eric Carle

183.   Eric Hill

184.   Maurice Sendak

185.   Dr Seuss

186.   Michael Bond

187.   Jeff Brown

188.   Roald Dahl

189.   Dick King-Smith

190.   Jeff Kinney

National Football League Teams

191.   Arizona

192.   Seattle

193.   Jacksonville

194.   Denver

195.   Pittsburgh

196.   Tennessee

197.   Detroit

198.   San Diego

199.   Buffalo

200.   Green Bay

Dog Breeds

201. Greyhound

202. St Bernard

203. Skye Terrier

204. The Old English Sheepdog

205. Rough Collie

206. English Pointer (although this is disputed)

207. Cairn Terrier

208. Dogue de Bordeaux

209. Great Dane

210. Beagle

Chemical Elements: Part 1

211. Lithium

212. Polonium

213. Carbon

214. Strontium

215. Iodine

216. Chlorine

217. Phosphorous

218. Nobelium

219. Bismuth

220. Palladium

Lead Singers: Part 1

221.   Ian Anderson

222.   Bruce Dickinson

223.   Ray Dorset

224.   Darren Hayes

225.   Ian Brown

226.   Billy Gibbons

227.   James Hetfield

228.   Jared Leto

229.   Phil Lynott

230.   Kevin Rowland

Games Consoles

231. Magnavox (Phillips also had a console named this)

232. Sony

233. Microsoft

234. Atari

235. Nintendo

236. Sega

237. Apple

238. Atari

239. Smith Engineering

240. SNK

City Nicknames

241. Edinburgh

242. Detroit

243. Dublin

244. Tehran

245. Vienna

246. Paris

247. Chicago

248. Hong Kong

249. Lima

250. Bolzano

Political Parties

251. UK Independence Party

252. Natural Law Party

253. Official Monster Raving Loony Party

254. Green Party

255. Liberal Democrats

256. Social Democratic and Labour Party

257. Sinn Fein

258. SDP

259. Conservative

260. Labour

Cartoon Baddies

261.   Dangermouse

262.   The Simpsons

263.   He-Man

264.   The Smurfs

265.   Dungeons and Dragons

266.   Battle of the Planets

267.   Count Duckula

268.   Inspector Gadget

269.   Transformers

270.   Thundercats

Sports à la Française

271. Waterskiing

272. Sailing

273. Ice skating

274. Wrestling

275. Archery

276. Boxing

277. Cycling

278. Swimming

279. Diving

280. Fishing

Film Decades

281.　1970s

282.　1940s

283.　2000s

284.　1990s

285.　1930s

286.　2010s

287.　1960s

288.　1980s

289.　1950s

290.　1920s

Young Animals: Part 1

291. Fawn

292. Kitten

293. Larva

294. Poult

295. Joey

296. Calf

297. Maggot

298. Gosling

299. Fry

300. Hatchling

Famous Albums: Part 1

301. Fleetwood Mac

302. Miles Davis

303. U2

304. The Beatles

305. Van Morrison

306. Rolling Stones

307. Nirvana

308. The Clash

309. Bob Dylan

310. Stevie Wonder

Detectives

311.   Doctor

312.   Forensic Pathologist

313.   Designer of Illusions for a magician

314.   DJ / Computer Expert

315.   Author

316.   Monk

317.   Retired 'Psychic'

318.   Antiques Dealer

319.   Lawyer

320.   Gardeners

Lakes

321. France

322. Italy

323. United Kingdom

324. Norway

325. Slovenia

326. Switzerland

327. Finland

328. Austria

329. Germany

330. Russia

American Presidents

331.   Ronald Reagan

332.   Harry S. Truman

333.   Gerald Ford

334.   Richard Nixon

335.   George W. Bush

336.   Andrew Johnson

337.   Thomas Jefferson

338.   James Madison

339.   Herbert Hoover

340.   Franklin D. Roosevelt

Original Languages

341. Swedish

342. French

343. Russian

344. German

345. Spanish

346. German

347. Czech

348. Japanese

349. English

350. French

Grand Prix Circuits

351.   United Kingdom

352.   Canada

353.   Germany

354.   Austria

355.   Japan

356.   South Africa

357.   Netherlands

358.   Mexico

359.   France

360.   United Arab Emirates

International Currencies: Part 1

361. Lev

362. Colon

363. Euro

364. Dollar

365. Ruble

366. Rand

367. Baht

368. Dong

369. Kwacha

370. Kroon

Measurements

371. Force

372. Electric Charge

373. Electrical Resistance

374. Magnetic Flux

375. Angle

376. Pressure

377. Inductance

378. Equivalent Dose of Ionising Radiation

379. Illuminance

380. Catalytic Activity

21st Century Song Lyrics

381.   Party in the USA

382.   Poker Face

383.   Thong Song

384.   Rock DJ

385.   I Kissed a Girl

386.   Still D.R.E.

387.   Survivor

388.   I Believe in a Thing Called Love

389.   Empire State of Mind

390.   Take Your Mama

Disney Songs

391. Snow White and the Seven Dwarfs

392. Dumbo

393. Pinocchio

394. Peter Pan

395. The Princess and the Frog

396. Robin Hood

397. The Little Mermaid

398. Beauty and the Beast

399. Aladdin

400. The Hunchback of Notre Dame

Internet Domains

401.   Austria

402.   Costa Rica

403.   Vanuatu

404.   Sweden

405.   Norway

406.   Monaco

407.   honduras

408.   Fiji

409.   Bulgaria

410.   South Africa

Greek Gods

411. Aphrodite

412. Hades (Pluto)

413. Hera

414. Poseidon

415. Zeus

416. Hestia

417. Hermes

418. Hephaestus

419. Dionysus

420. Demeter

Year of Publication

421.   1962

422.   1847

423.   1960

424.   1937

425.   1897

426.   1884

427.   1951

428.   1954

429.   2003

430.   1865

Cars: Part 1

431. Renault

432. Vauxhall

433. Jeep

434. Porsche

435. Honda

436. Citroen

437. Fiat

438. Volkswagon

439. FSO

440. Pontiac

Major League Baseball

441.   Atlanta

442.   Boston

443.   Pittsburgh

444.   Texas

445.   Milwaukee

446.   Seattle

447.   St Louis

448.   Baltimore

449.   Miami

450.   Toronto

Chemical Elements: Part 2

451. Lead

452. Copper

453. Potassium

454. Tin

455. Sodium

456. Flourine

457. Iron

458. Manganese

459. Krypton

460. Hydrogen

Food Songs

461. The Beatles

462. Tori Amos

463. Bow Wow Wow

464. Billie Holiday

465. Lieutenant Pigeon

466. Don McLean

467. Fats Domino

468. The Rolling Stones

469. Streetband

470. Def Lepard

Great Works of Art

471.   Sandro Botticelli

472.   Claude Monet

473.   Rembrandt van Rijn

474.   Edvard Munch

475.   Johannes Vermeer

476.   Pablo Picasso

477.   Michelangelo

478.   Leonardo da Vinci

479.   Vincent van Gogh

480.   Salvador Dali

Capital Cities of Asia

481. Cambodia

482. Laos

483. Nepal

484. Bhutan

485. Mongolia

486. North Korea

487. Taiwan

488. Myanmar

489. East Timor

490. Sri Lanka

Leaders' Wives

491. Lyndon B Johnson

492. George Washington

493. James A. Garfield

494. Abraham Lincoln

495. Calvin Coolidge

496. John Quincy Adams

497. Jimmy Carter

498. Theodore Roosevelt

499. John F. Kennedy

500. Barack Obama

Anagrams: Part 1

501.   Stephen King

502.   Agatha Christie

503.   Ernest Hemingway

504.   William Shakespeare

505.   George RR Martin

506.   Oscar Wilde

507.   Jackie Collins

508.   Edgar Allan Poe

509.   Jane Austen

510.   Charles Dickens

Winter Olympic Sports

511.   Skeleton

512.   Bobsleigh

513.   Nordic Combined

514.   Curling

515.   Biathlon

516.   Alpine Skiing

517.   Ski Jumping

518.   Luge

519.   Ice Hockey

520.   Figure Skating

Museums

521. Netherlands

522. Spain

523. Mexico City

524. Taipei

525. Italy

526. USA

527. France

528. United Kingdom

529. Germany

530. Austria

Measuring Devices

531.   Humidity

532.   Time

533.   Vertical distance

534.   Ocean depth

535.   Air pressure

536.   Wind speed

537.   Gas pressure

538.   Colour

539.   Distance travelled

540.   Blood pressure

Famous Albums: Part 2

541.   Curtis Mayfield

542.   Public Enemy

543.   The Zombies

544.   David Bowie

545.   Captain Beefheart and His Magic Band

546.   Patti Smith

547.   The Jimi Hendrix Experience

548.   Bob Marley and the Wailers

549.   Love

550.   Radiohead

Flag Carriers

551. Panama

552. United Arab Emirates

553. Ireland

554. Columbia

555. Russia

556. Bahrain

557. Israel

558. Australia

559. Latvia

560. Spain

Volcanoes

561. Ecuador

562. Tanzania

563. Peru

564. Mexico

565. Turkey

566. USA (Alaska)

567. Japan

568. Italy

569. Canada

570. Russia

Leaders in War

571.   USA - WWII

572.   Union - American Civil War

573.   Confederates - American Civil War

574.   Japan - WWII

575.   USA - Persian Gulf War

576.   Carthage - First Punic War

577.   Persia - Battle of Pasargadae

578.   Macedon - Campaings in Persia, Syria and Egypt

579.   France - Napoleonic Wars

580.   Normans - Battle of Hastings

Authors

581. Jane Austen

582. Miguel de Cervantes

583. F. Scott Fitzgerald

584. John Steinbeck

585. Leo Tolstoy

586. Adolf Hitler

587. Jonathan Swift

588. Geoffrey Chaucer

589. Herman Melville

590. Franz Kafka

Previously Known As...

591. Michael Caine

592. Woody Allen

593. Harry Houdini

594. George Michael

595. Natalie Portman

596. Judy Garland

597. Stevie Wonder

598. Katy Perry

599. Marilyn Monroe

600. Whoopi Goldberg

Olympic Cities

601.   Montreal

602.   Moscow

603.   Athens

604.   Rome

605.   Berlin

606.   London

607.   Oslo

608.   Paris

609.   Amsterdam

610.   Seoul

SI Units

611. Ampere

612. Watt

613. Second

614. Kilogram

615. Becquerel

616. Kelvin

617. Metre

618. Hertz

619. Tesla

620. Farad

Nationalities of Singers

621. Russia

622. Australian

623. Icelandic

624. New Zealand

625. German

626. Greek

627. Jamaican

628. Indian

629. Senegalese

630. South Korean

Famous Battles

631. 490 BC

632. 1066

633. 1704

634. 331 BC

635. 1815

636. 1942

637. 1863

638. 732

639. 1916

640. 1415

Nicknames of Countries

641. England

642. Ukraine

643. China

644. Sri Lanka

645. New Zealand

646. Egypt

647. Madagascar

648. Ireland

649. USA

650. Iceland

Mythical Creatures

651. Minotaur

652. Pegasus

653. Centaur

654. The Gorgons

655. Cyclops

656. Cerberus

657. Gryphon

658. Sirens

659. Sphinx

660. Echidna

Literary Characters: Part 1

661. Tinker, Tailor, Soldier, Spy

662. Harry Potter and the Philosopher's Stone

663. 1984

664. The Jungle Book

665. The Lord of the Rings

666. The Hitchhiker's Guide to the Galaxy

667. The Importance of Being Earnest

668. Moby Dick

669. The Canterbury Tales

670. The Hunger Games

Team Numbers

671. 11

672. 5

673. 15

674. 4

675. 7

676. 11

677. 6

678. 8

679. 15

680. 10

Horror Movies

681. A Nightmare on Elm Street

682. Texas Chainsaw Massacre

683. Hellraiser

684. Friday the 13th

685. The Omen

686. Halloween

687. Psycho

688. The Ring

689. House of 1000 Corpses

690. IT

Moons

691. Earth

692. Mars

693. Jupiter

694. Jupiter

695. Saturn

696. Saturn

697. Uranus

698. Neptune

699. Pluto

700. Uranus

Notes and Keys

701.   One half

702.   2

703.   4

704.   One eighth

705.   1

706.   Sharps: F

707.   Flats: B, E, A, D, G, C

708.   Sharps: F, C, G, D

709.   Flats: B, E

710.   Flats: B, E, A

Movie Taglines

711. Alien

712. The Fly

713. Cool Runnings

714. Close Encounters of the Third Kind

715. Braveheart

716. Taxi Driver

717. Jaws 2

718. The Prestige

719. 12 Monkeys

720. Independence Day

State Capitals

721. Annapolis

722. Springfield

723. Tallahassee

724. Salem

725. Baton Rouge

726. Phoenix

727. Honolulu

728. Austin

729. Salt Lake City

730. Lincoln

Parliament Buildings

731. Netherlands

732. Democratic Republic of the Congo

733. France

734. Germany

735. India

736. Ireland

737. Trinidad and Tobago

738. Denmark

739. China

740. Namibia

Eras of Art

741. Italian Renaissance

742. Cubism

743. Pre-Raphaelite Brotherhood

744. Realism

745. Dutch Golden Age (Baroque)

746. Neoclassicism

747. Dadaism

748. Rococo

749. Impressionism

750. Romanticism

Acronyms

751.   Major League Baseball

752.   Own Goal

753.   Ladies Professional Golf Association

754.   International Olympic Committee

755.   Fédération Internationale de Football Association

756.   Did Not Finish

757.   Average

758.   Technical Knockout

759.   Cross Country

760.   Quarterback

Serial Killers

761.   The Acid Bath Murderer

762.   Doctor Death

763.   The Happy Face Killer

764.   The Butcher of Plainfield

765.   The Brooklyn Vampire

766.   Citizen X

767.   The Moors Murderers

768.   The Killer Clown

769.   The Yorkshire Ripper

770.   The Boston Strangler

Moonwalkers

771.   Apollo 15

772.   Apollo 15

773.   Apollo 14

774.   Apollo 12

775.   Apollo 12

776.   Apollo 11

777.   Apollo 16

778.   Apollo 17

779.   Apollo 16

780.   Apollo 17

Symphonies

781. Berlioz

782. Liszt

783. Schubert

784. Haydn

785. Mozart

786. Mahler

787. Beethoven

788. Shostakovich

789. Vaughan Williams

790. Tchaikovsky

Sitcoms

791. Milwaukee, Wisconsin

792. Scranton, Pennsylvania

793. Lanford (Fictional), Illinois

794. Quahog (Fictional), Rhode Island

795. Seattle, Washington

796. Boston, Massachusetts

797. Torquay, Devon

798. New York

799. Peckham, London

800. Uijeongbu, South Korea

Famous Landmarks

801.   New York

802.   Paris

803.   Copenhagen

804.   Agra

805.   Rio de Janeiro

806.   Istanbul

807.   Barcelona

808.   Brussels

809.   The Vatican City

810.   Jerusalem

Calendar Dates

811. November the 11th

812. March the 15th

813. January the 1st

814. January the 26th

815. April the 23rd

816. May the 4th

817. July the 1st

818. October the 31st

819. November the 5th

820. February the 14th

Bible Quotes

821. Genesis

822. Exodus

823. Gospel According to Luke

824. Gospel According to John

825. 1 Corinthians

826. Proverbs

827. The Book of Psalms

828. Philippians

829. Deuteronomy

830. Gospel According to Matthew

Winter Olympics

831. St Moritz

832. Sochi

833. Salt Lake City

834. Lillehammer

835. Calgary

836. Sarajevo

837. Innsbruck

838. Oslo

839. Chamonix

840. Vancouver

Cars: Part 2

841.   Mitsubishi

842.   Aston Martin

843.   Cadillac

844.   Dodge

845.   Ferrari

846.   Jaguar

847.   Lamborghini

848.   Land Rover

849.   Jensen

850.   Renault

Scientists

851.   Sir Isaac Newton

852.   Werner Heisenberg

853.   Einstein

854.   Charles Darwin

855.   Johannes Kepler

856.   Archimedes

857.   Sir Alexander Fleming

858.   Michael Faraday

859.   Frederick Banting

860.   Marie Curie

Songs with Colours

861. New Order

862. Procol Harum

863. The Stranglers

864. Nena

865. Jimi Hendrix

866. R.E.M.

867. Split Enz

868. Cream

869. Soundgarden

870. Fats Domino

Archenemies

871. Aquaman

872. Daredevil

873. The X-Men

874. Batman

875. Superman

876. Captain America

877. The Fantastic Four

878. Thor

879. Iron Man

880. Green Lantern

Rivers

881.   Potomac

882.   Plate

883.   Danube

884.   Yellow River

885.   Thames

886.   Seine

887.   Tigris

888.   Tiber

889.   Amstel

890.   Nile

European Monarchs

891. Albert II

892. Margrethe II

893. Hans-Adam II

894. Jean

895. Rainier III

896. Beatrix

897. Harald V

898. Juan Carlos I

899. Carl XVI Gustaf

900. Elizabeth II

Opening Lines

901.   Pride and Prejudice

902.   A Tale of Two Cities

903.   1984

904.   Finnegans Wake

905.   The Great Gatsby

906.   Moby Dick

907.   Peter Pan

908.   Slaughterhouse Five

909.   Harry Potter and the Philosopher's Stone

910.   Fear and Loathing in Las Vegas

Movie Characters

911. The Godfather

912. Psycho

913. Alien

914. One Flew Over the Cuckoo's Nest

915. Withnail and I

916. The Wizard of Oz

917. Taxi Driver

918. Wall Street

919. Pulp Fiction

920. A Clockword Orange

Sports Trophies

921. Ice Hockey

922. Bowls

923. American Football

924. Tennis

925. Rugby Union

926. Indycar Racing

927. Golf

928. Sailing

929. Cricket

930. Fencing

Phobias

931. Spiders

932. Darnkess

933. Fish

934. Birds

935. Beards

936. Shadows

937. Lakes

938. Enclosed places

939. Ghosts

940. Cats

Sporting Locations

941.   Horse Racing (Kentucky Derby)

942.   Motor Racing (Indy 500)

943.   Tennis (Wimbledon Championships)

944.   Horse Racing (Grand National)

945.   Golf (Various)

946.   Golf (Masters)

947.   Football (Various)

948.   Motor Racing (24 Hours)

949.   Sailing (Cowes Week)

950.   F1 Grand Prix

Inventions

951. Alexander Graham Bell

952. Tim Berners-Lee

953. Eli Whitney

954. James Watt

955. Johann Gutenberg

956. John Logie Baird

957. Benjamin Franklin

958. James Hargreaves

959. Christopher Cockerell

960. Percy Shaw

Deserts

961. United Kingdom

962. Ukraine

963. Australia

964. Spain

965. Chile and Peru

966. Botswana, Namibia and South Africa

967. Mongolia and China

968. Israel

969. Pakistan

970. Argentina and Chile

Revolutionaries

971.   Turkey

972.   Scotland

973.   China

974.   Iran

975.   Ireland

976.   England

977.   Italy

978.   Cuba

979.   India

980.   France

Anagrams: Part 2

981.   Sherlock Holmes

982.   Lord Peter Wimsey

983.   Columbo

984.   Miss Marple

985.   Inspector Clouseau

986.   Hercule Poirot

987.   Sam Spade

988.   Endeavour Morse

989.   Cordelia Gray

990.   Father Brown

Famous Olympians

991. Fencing

992. Weightlifting

993. Archery

994. Rowing

995. Judo

996. Swimming

997. Sailing

998. Gymnastics

999. Cycling

1000. Canoeing

Gemstones

1001. Green

1002. Blue

1003. White (with a blue tinge)

1004. Purple

1005. Red

1006. Black

1007. Green

1008. Yellow

1009. Blue

1010. Red

Young Animals: Part 2

1011. Kit

1012. Nymph

1013. Cria

1014. Cygnet

1015. Cub

1016. Leveret

1017. Foal

1018. Eyas

1019. Kid

1020. Elver

Musical Nicknames

1021. Johnny Logan

1022. Ozzy Osborne

1023. Ray Davies

1024. James Brown

1025. Harry Belafonte

1026. Michael Jackson

1027. Bruce Springsteen

1028. Dame Vera Lynn

1029. Benny Goodman

1030. Paul Weller

Bridges

1031. New York

1032. Venice

1033. Mostar

1034. Prague

1035. London

1036. San Francisco

1037. Lisbon

1038. Florence

1039. Canon City

1040. Isfahan

Countries and Capitals

1041. Brussels

1042. Beijing

1043. Zagreb

1044. Copenhagen

1045. Berlin

1046. Reykjavík

1047. Jakarta

1048. Seoul

1049. Lima

1050. Ankara

Roman Gods

1051. Minerva

1052. Vesta

1053. Juno

1054. Ceres

1055. Diana

1056. Venus

1057. Mars

1058. Neptune

1059. Vulcan

1060. Jupiter

Literary Characters: Part 2

1061. Great Expectations

1062. The Princess Bride

1063. Lolita

1064. Catch 22

1065. To Kill a Mockingbird

1066. The Wind in the Willows

1067. Pride and Prejudice

1068. Anne of Green Gables

1069. Trainspotting

1070. The Shining

International Currencies: Part 2

1071. Dinar

1072. Real

1073. Krone

1074. Quetzal

1075. Rupee

1076. Yen

1077. Won

1078. Ringgit

1079. Zloty

1080. Shilling

World Cup Hosts

1081. Argentina

1082. England

1083. Switzerland

1084. Chile

1085. France

1086. Uruguay

1087. South Africa

1088. Mexico

1089. Brazil

1090. South Korea & Japan

Chemical Elements: Part 3

1091. Mercury

1092. Einsteinium

1093. Ytterbium

1094. Arsenic

1095. Antimony

1096. Barium

1097. Tungsten

1098. Plutonium

1099. Hassium

1100. Silver

90s Lyrics

1101. Cotton Eye Joe

1102. No Scrubs

1103. Informer

1104. Genie in a Bottle

1105. Kiss From A Rose

1106. What's My Age Again

1107. Goldeneye

1108. Wind of Change

1109. Boom! Shake The Room

1110. Here Comes The Hotstepper

Country Names

1111. Japan

1112. Greenland

1113. Germany

1114. Sweden

1115. Finland

1116. Austria

1117. Croatia

1118. Seychelles

1119. Fiji

1120. Hungary

African Capitals

1121. Ethiopia

1122. Senegal

1123. Uganda

1124. Somalia

1125. Algeria

1126. Tanzania

1127. Zimbabwe

1128. Kenya

1129. Sierra Leone

1130. Morocco

Famous Leaders

1131. Germany

1132. Tibet

1133. Roman Empire

1134. Turkey

1135. Mongol Empire

1136. Carolingian Empire (although King of the Franks or King of Italy are also correct)

1137. Prussia

1138. Egypt and Syria

1139. The Hunnic Empire

1140. Babylon

Children's Books: Part 2

1141. A A Milne

1142. Jill Murphy

1143. E B White

1144. Eoin Colfer

1145. Clive King

1146. C S Lewis

1147. Mary Norton

1148. J K Rowling

1149. Richard Adams

1150. Anthony Horowitz

Football Nicknames

1151. Sheffield United

1152. Bournemouth

1153. Exeter City

1154. Arsenal

1155. Sheffield Wednesday

1156. Bristol Rovers

1157. Peterborough United

1158. Crewe Alexandra

1159. Brighton & Hove Albion

1160. Ipswich Town

Computer Acronyms

1161. American Standard Code for Information Interchange

1162. Beginner's All-purpose Symbolic Instruction Code

1163. Central Processing Unit

1164. Domain Name System

1165. Graphical User Interface

1166. HyperText Transfer Protocol

1167. Instant Message

1168. Peer To Peer

1169. Personal Computer

1170. Universal Serial Bus

Collective Nouns

1171. Shrewdness or Troop

1172. Sounder

1173. Army

1174. Pod, School or Team

1175. Pride or Sawt

1176. Parliament

1177. Nest

1178. Descent

1179. Murder

1180. Pack

Lead Singers: Part 2

1181. AC/DC

1182. Right Said Fred

1183. Green Day

1184. Muse

1185. Pulp

1186. Dire Straits

1187. Babylon Zoo

1188. Wet Wet Wet

1189. No Doubt

1190. Aerosmith

Catchphrases

1191. Take Me Out

1192. The Dick Emery Show

1193. Dad's Army

1194. Steptoe and Son

1195. Allo 'Allo

1196. Harry Enfield's Television Programme

1197. Little Britain

1198. Mastermind

1199. Red Dwarf

1200. Crackerjack

You may also enjoy...